The Strongest One of All

a Korean folktale

retold by Y. Kim Choi • illustrated by Stephano Vitale

HARCOURT BRACE & COMPANY

Orlando Atlanta Austin Boston San Francisco Chicago Dallas New York
Toronto London

Once upon a time in a small village, there lived a father mouse and a mother mouse.

They had a beautiful daughter whom they loved very much. They wanted her to marry the strongest one of all.

So they left the village. They went far to find the strongest one of all.

They went up the hill and met Sun. They asked, "Oh, strongest one, will you marry our daughter?"

But Sun said, "I am not the strongest. When Cloud comes, I can not shine."

They went down the hill and met Cloud. They asked, "Oh, strongest one, will you marry our daughter?"

But Cloud said, "I am not the strongest. When Wind blows, I can not keep still."

They went over the lake and met Wind. They asked, "Oh, strongest one, will you marry our daughter?"

But Wind said, "I am not the strongest. When Statue sits, I can not move him."

They went along the beach and met Statue. They asked, "Oh, strongest one, will you marry our daughter?"

But Statue said, "I am not the strongest. When a mouse digs a hole under my feet, I will fall."

So the father mouse and the mother mouse went back to the village. There they found a kind mouse who wanted to marry their daughter.